IT'S
TIME
TO TELL
MY STORY

A CHILD'S ESCAPE FROM CAMBODIA'S POL POT REGIME

JOYCE BOLENDER
AS TOLD BY VANY NOP

PREFACE

History and the world know about Phnom Penh, Cambodia. That is where Pol Pot from 1975 to 1979 orchestrated the "killing fields," mass burial sites where people were taken and killed with metal objects, knives, nails and hammers, since bullets were "too expensive." Some people were burned alive. These murders were committed at night, and loud propaganda music was played to cover the screams of the people.

Children and infants were removed from their mothers and smashed against the Chankiri tree, often for the guards' grand amusement. The estimate is that one-fourth of the Cambodian population in 1975 were killed. The atrocities were compared to the nazi murders for the purpose of ethnic cleansing, forced disappearances, forced labor, and senseless murder.

The targets for the genocide were previous military (including my father), political leaders, journalists, students, intellectuals, business leaders, doctors, lawyers, all ethnic minorities, and religious groups.

The goals were ultra-nationalism, Marxist dogma, anti-intellectualism, racism, xenophobia, to name a few. They, like the Nazis, wanted to create a "master race." However, the way they did it was to systematically persecute and kill the educated, keeping the peasants for forced labor.

Since my brothers were intelligent, educated, and/or religious members of their community, they would be at the top of the list for genocide. That would explain their disappearance. It is a blessing that my baby sister died before the regime could take her and destroy her small body for someone's amusement. Burying her was a tragedy but worse would have been for her to be in the hands of the Khmer Rouge.

My family was one of the millions affected by this time, and I lived to tell my story.

INTRODUCTION

In 1979 The Catholic Diocese in Richmond, Virginia, took a stand to aid refugees from SE Asia, after the Vietnamese War came to a muddled end. They decided that the greatest help they could provide was to resettle the many young survivors of the war. They established a plan to create foster homes for these young kids, give them a stable environment, an education, English classes, and help them meet their physical and emotional needs as they adjusted to another culture, religion, and language. They brought with them the memories, the losses, and the nightmares of living through this catastrophic period in history.

Roanoke, Virginia, had opened an office, and Joyce, who would become my American mother, became the director of the program there. She began advertising for foster homes, and the response was rewarding.

The program was called Refugee Unaccompanied Minors Program (RUMP), and teens from Laos, Cambodia, and Vietnam arrived from Thailand and moved into American homes, enrolling in local schools and being assigned a social worker to help them through the adjustments. A psychiatrist was on board to focus on mental health concerns that might occur. Counselors from their individual countries were assigned to help them with the language and cultural barriers and to help them feel less isolated from their country and culture.

The program offered many cultural activities that the youths themselves planned and performed or participated in. The group was very cohesive, and, overall, everyone adjusted well to the program. Many expressed their appreciation for the chance to begin a life in the United States, and most went on to lead productive, satisfactory lives.

MY NOTES

Dith Pran, *Children of Cambodia's Killing Fields: Memoirs by Survivors,* states:

> It is important to me that the new generation of Cambodians and the Cambodian Americans become active and tell the world what happened to them and their families…I want them to never forget the faces of their relatives and friends who were killed during that time. The dead are crying out for justice.

I was only eight when things collapsed in my world. Until then, I enjoyed a good life and the love of a supportive family. We were comfortable, never having to worry about food or other necessities. We could have what we needed as well as what we wanted. What I eventually endured and survived has affected my life in many ways.

During the turmoil and genocide of my country and most of my family, I became acutely aware of my *will to survive*. It made me appreciate family. It gave me a strong desire to make my life mean something. For me and the family I had to leave behind in

Cambodia, I am thankful every day that I was able to survive with my brother, Kha.

Over the years, I have thought many times about telling my story. When my American mother, Joyce, asked me recently if I had ever felt a need to tell my experiences during that time of Pol Pot, I eagerly told her I had. For many years, I wanted to tell the story, but I had neither the encouragement nor the help to do so. With her encouragement and commitment to help me, we began this journey of loss, sadness, determination, and sharing of my history and my past, so I can find peace in my future.

I also want it to motivate my children and grandchildren to learn their Cambodian history, not to lose it to indifference, and to remember and cherish the names of my lost family. Their names need to be spoken, so we can keep them alive in our minds and hearts. By doing this, we can bring some degree of justice. They will always be remembered.

JUST A SMALL BOY

I started life in a close family of five boys. My father, Yen Nop, was a general in the king's army, and my mother, Sue Nop, owned and oversaw several businesses in Phnom Penh at the lower center of Cambodia. Being the capitol of Cambodia, Phnom Penh swirled with activity, bustling growth, and endless many opportunities for everyone.

My family were considered upper middle class, owning and managing businesses. My father had earned status as a general in the army.

We had a beautiful condo, one of about eighteen floors in the building. We were on the top floor, with five bedrooms, two baths, a large kitchen, a living room, and access to the rooftop penthouse-type area.

A woman helped with cleaning, cooking, and caring for me while my mother managed and fostered the success of her businesses. We called our helper "Auntie." She was warm and kind, and she gave me pretty much whatever I wanted.

Even though we had a large condo with all those bedrooms, we usually slept on the living room floor. My mother stored many supplies for her business in the bedrooms.

It was a good life for a six or seven year old, and I played on the roof a lot, shared playtime at the temple with my brothers, had friends, and never had a concern about anything. I rode my bike on the roof area as it wasn't safe to ride or play on the busy streets.

I really enjoyed stopping in the market to get some favorite foods. One of my favorite foods was kuy teav (rice with either beef, chicken, shrimp, or vegetable noodle soup). I loved seafood, and we ate a lot of fish. Auntie often took me shopping at the markets, and I liked visiting my mother at her general store located in the area mall called NEW STORE. They sold food, clothes, and many other items. The store was always busy.

My brother, Suen, owned and ran a movie theater called Sorajay, right across the street from my mother's store. I spent many happy hours there. Bruce Lee was popular then, and we saw all of his movies, as well as other SE Asian movies.

I was good at entertaining myself, going to daycare, stopping at the temple to see Vana. We would play games until time to go home. I had other toys and a slingshot that I practiced using all day long, not knowing it would one day help me to survive.

Life was simple and good for a small boy, innocent and confident and well loved by my mother and brothers.

My father, a general in the Cambodian Army, was seldom in our home. He was a tough officer and spent little time with us kids. He stayed mostly with his Army buddies, and if one of us boys would try to talk to him, he would push or send us away, having no interest in talking to or spending time with any of us. My father especially ignored me, the youngest, but my brothers gave me the attention I needed.

My mother was very strong, independent, and organized. She seemed to have a good mind for business because she was in control of all the business operations and was successful with it. I was unaware of the business dynamics. I was a small boy, and life for me was playing, eating, and sleeping. Not a care in the world, like any seven year old. What did I know about what would lie ahead?

FAMILY

In a strong patriarchal family, my mother was independent but compliant with the expectations of the times for women in SE Asia. Being the youngest, I received a lot of attention and felt the love of my mother and brothers. With my dad usually away in the military, my mother held the family together.

My oldest brother was Son. He was about thirteen years older than me. He eventually helped my mother with the business until the war hit, and he then disappeared into the unknown, fleeing the murderous reign coming toward us. Around his age of twenty-one, rumor circulated by a friend of my father that Son had been killed.

Next came my brother Suen, who was about seven years older than me. I have few memories of him and know only that, like Son, he had escaped to the countryside when Pol Pot moved his troops to our area of the country. Likewise, his whereabouts are unknown. He and Son fled together. I hope they were able to watch out for each other as they moved away from the dreaded onslaught.

My next brother was Vana, five years older than me. He had become a Buddhist monk, and we often went to visit him after school. We sat in classes at WAT SWAYKOM (temple) and learned about Buddhism, meditation, and how to be gracious and kind to people. That was instilled in me very early. I loved going to the temple, and I have good memories of that time in my life. I have no idea what happened to Vana when the struggles began. Pol Pot did not like the Buddhist monks, so I suppose Vana met the same fate as the others.

My last brother was Kha, four years older than me. We spent a lot of time together. I can remember my mother walking the two of us to school each day before she went to work. After school, often she would take us to the temple to see Vana and to worship there.

My mother was the center of our family. She always had a smile, she enjoyed the company of friends and good business acquaintances. She was a good mother who sang to us and took us to temple often to pray.

I do not remember any grandparents, aunts or uncles, cousins, or other family. Of course, I was very small, and memories of that time are lost in the shadows of a small boy's recollection. The powers of those happy memories after that peaceful time are gone, and the horrors of my life began to take place when I was around seven. At around eight years of age, I began the flight of my life.

POLITICS

Pol Pot became the brutal communist dictator of Cambodia around April of 1975 and started by taking control of the capital, Phnom Penh, which was when his Khmer Rouge regime began. I was about seven then.

Pol Pot came from a family of farmers and was smart. His goal was to have a classless agrarian society. To do that, he rid the country of doctors, teachers, monks, religious and political leaders, even people that wore glasses.

Anyone and everyone presented a threat to the dictator, and he wasted no time deliberately killing the vast majority of his citizens by shooting, beheading, and torturing them. Like Germany, we had our own holocaust.

The army soon joined forces with the Khmer Rouge when the king decided to acquiesce to the dictator's agenda. The king had exiled to China, but he snuck back into the country and merged his troops with the Khmer Rouge.

My father – and others in the army – were expected to fight against the country he loved. As Pol Pot began to rule, he did so with an iron fist and with evil intent. The movie *The Killing Fields* graphically showed the horrors that were inflicted on all the people who might try to object to his rule.

Even if some people might be willing to be part of the regime, Pol Pot methodically killed those who were educated, had political power, or were everyday average people. If he considered they posed a threat to him, he gave no second thought to annihilating them.

The Khmer Rouge were great record keepers. They were very diligent about knowing the exact number of citizens in prison and those who had been executed. They methodically took our names, where we were from, our ages, and our family ties. They knew how many bodies were in each of the graves at the killing fields.

Many of the soldiers in the army, like my father, fled the military and changed from their uniforms and boots into peasant clothes to become invisible, fading into the jungles and forests to avoid detection. They dropped their guns where they stood and left everything behind them. Few of them lived to tell about their ordeal.

According to a friend of my father, who told me when I was around eight that I needed to leave the area, that he had witnessed the Khmer Rouge beheading my father, that he was not coming back, and we were on our own. (I later heard that 80 percent of the king's army were slaughtered).

The North Vietnamese were using the Ho Che Minh Trail to move supplies, weapons, and other things. The United States sent troops and planes to stop their advance. The plan was to bomb the trail, but apparently they received the wrong information and bombed the town, killing many civilians. I witnessed that bombing.

That was the beginning of the horror I would live for the next several years as I struggled to stay alive. I saw it in my nightmares for many years thereafter.

FLEEING

The history books have the facts, but I have the details of life during this time. For a small boy who had lived a normal life, suddenly that life of peace and tranquility was gone. In its place were horrors that still shadow me at fifty-five years of age.

After the killings began, all that was left of my family was my mother, then three months pregnant with my little sister, Kha, and me. I was about eight then, and Kha was about twelve. When word came to our community that Pol Pot and his troops were heading toward Phnom Penh, my father told my mother that we needed to leave NOW, to go to safety, that it was time for the three of us to flee.

We had no time to pack anything. My father arranged for a helicopter to come to the roof, pick us up, and take us away. The helicopter arrived but couldn't land on the roof, and the army shot it down.

Then my mother gathered us together, and we left, running with thousands of others, trying to escape the troops. I saw my mother as my savior and followed her blindly.

Once the fleeing began, it was like a herd of cattle racing through the jungle and into the countryside. We were like a colony of ants, millions of them, racing away from death into the unknown. I often said during that time that I wanted to live and would die trying.

If someone fell, the others ran over them. No one stopped to help, no one even thought to slow down or reach out a hand. I saw little kids get trampled as everyone was running for their lives. As we ran, troops were everywhere, shooting at us, killing those they caught.

I remember running and seeing a small two-year-old girl sitting beside her dead mother, crying. I wanted to stop and help her, but my mother pulled me away, telling me, "Come on! Come on! We have to go!"

As we ran, we saw dead bodies everywhere, infants on the ground, crying and screaming. The bodies were in various conditions from the stabbings, beheadings, beatings, and shootings. My mother told us not to look but keep running. So I tried to do what she said.

My mother insisted she would lead the way and that Kha and I were to follow her. She was very firm about this, and we listened and obeyed. I believe she felt if there was danger, she would protect us by leading the way. She remained strong the entire trip, even when her body was weak, swollen, and heavy with our little sister. Mother's strength gave us courage.

At first, we zigzagged through the country, running through small villages to avoid the military. After a week of this, my mother decided it would be safer to take our chances and head for the border, so we did.

Fear was always a part of our life, and we had to swallow it to keep moving. There were mines, trip wires, and bamboo holes that were always a threat as we moved northwest toward the border.

Let me tell you about the bamboo holes. Soldiers would dig a big, deep hole, then they would carve the end of a bamboo rod to a sharp point and place the rod firmly upright in the hole. They would cover the hole with leaves or whatever. Then, when someone would step into the hole, they would be impaled.

There was no food available, so we had to find something to eat. We ate snakes, fish, crickets, birds, frogs, lizards (there were a lot of lizards there), bird's eggs or some we stole from a farm along the way, leaves, grass.

We would get our water from the rice fields or a puddle in the road where a buffalo might have trampled. We were careful to use a cloth to filter what we drank for fear of getting disease. However, it did not stop the constant diarrhea we experienced.

We often saw cobras, boas, anacondas, snakes of all kinds, tigers, wild boars, tarantulas, lots of spiders. The terror around me made a snake crawling up my arm no distraction. I would brush it off and go back to sleep.

Along the way, we found some shelter, living in empty sheds that offered some cover. The sheds were flimsy structures made of leaves and bamboo stalks with leaves for a roof. It was a temporary site for the farmers to use when taking livestock out to graze in what had been rice fields but now were dormant because of the war. The sheds were not permanent or sturdy, but they served a purpose of protecting us to a degree.

The villagers did not want us there, and often when Kha and I went out to search for something to eat, they would gang up on us and beat us. Or throw rocks at us.

So we were often reluctant to go out in the day time. However, going at night limited us and what we could find. We found ourselves moving on to the next village and finding the next shed. Our mother, then quite pregnant, had trouble moving. But she did not give up.

We all pushed forward until it was time for the baby to be born. We came to a small village, and I would run into the center twenty times a day to beg for food, each time being turned away. They told me they had no food either.

On one trip, I met a young woman who offered help. She and her new husband had little, but they felt sorry for us, and they shared the use of their shed and provided some food for us.

When my mother began to give birth, a doctor-like man came to the shed and helped her deliver my baby sister. I don't remember her name. She was covered with a rash, like chickenpox, she cried often, and there was no milk to give her.

Mother was too weak to do anything, so Kha and I cooked. Once, Kha burned our meal, and my mother told me that I would be in charge of the cooking. Kha was in charge of other things since he was bigger. We slept in a shed with Kha against the wall, my mother next to him, the baby next to me, and I slept in front of the door.

Eventually, my mother became very sick, her body was swollen, and when the baby was two months old, my mother died. Kha and I, with some help from a villager passing by, carried my mother into the forest. Kha and I dug a hole and buried her there.

We then had this tiny baby to take care of, and I wasn't far from being a baby myself. A woman in one of the villages took us in to help until the baby died. But I grew up fast in that time and place.

When the baby died, Kha and I took her to the woods and buried her there. We together dug a shallow hole since she was so small, and we placed her there. There were tears, but we had no choice.

As we moved to the next village and the next, Kha and I stayed close to the swarm of people fleeing toward the border like us. If we tried to join someone, we were quickly pushed away. It was the consensus that too many in a group would draw attention, so the two of us moved forward with no contact with anyone else.

I felt driven to move and I wanted to live. I was willing to take any risk, walk any path to get to the border. We always headed north, following the sun because, as we moved through the villages and asked for directions to Thailand, they would say "It's 40 kilometers ahead" or 25 kilometers ahead," and they assured us we were going the right way.

We often had to use a slingshot to kill for food. Or a rock or some sticks from the woods. We would beg for matches from the villagers (many smoked so they had access to matches), so we could cook the fish we caught or small animals or insects like crickets. I was so hungry I would have eaten dirt.

As we moved closer to Thailand, Pol Pot moved his troops there. We saw bombs going off and heard bullets zooming by. I could feel the heat of a bullet whizzing by my head. I could smell the burn from the bullet as it rushed past me. The troops were everywhere, on all sides.

There were dead bodies everywhere. Some had been dead for a long time, and the stench made me sick. We saw skeletons scattered where they fell, and it became second nature to see such sites and not have them register in my young brain what it all meant. But terror was a constant in every breath we took.

Mines were everywhere. As we walked, we often witnessed someone stepping on a mine and being blown up, their flesh and brains flying into the air. At times, pieces of flesh would fall on my face or head or a part of my body. I became numb to this. But the feeling of terror never went away.

Walking through the woods, the thought of mines was always in my head. But, after a while, trying to anticipate where one might be just slowed us down and became too much of a burden to worry about anymore. So I tried to remove the thought from my mind. But the fear stayed there.

We found it better to travel during the day. The main reason was because we could see what lay ahead. At night, we could not see anything and basically had to feel our way forward. We decided, despite the risks of being in the open during daylight, it was safer than trying to move at night.

No matter when we walked, there was always the risk of stepping on mines or being shot at. I remember feeling a bullet whiz past my head, but we kept moving forward. There was no time to stop and hide. The border was our goal, and we were determined to get there. So I wiped it from my mind and kept moving.

Eighty percent of the terrain was jungle. There were many palm trees, and the land was flat with mountains far in the distance. Fortunately, we were not running during the monsoon. We had rain but not in abundance. It was hot and mucky all the time, even at night. There were many mosquitoes and insects, too. We began our running sometime in March, and the monsoons usually didn't hit until September.

One night a few months after my mother died, we were lying in the shed on a dark night. I looked up, and there in the doorway stood my mother. I called to Kha, and he saw her, too. I think she came to let us know she was OK and to check on us one last time to make sure that we were OK. I did feel comforted and less afraid for a few seconds.

THE CONCENTRATION CAMP

Leaving home and arriving at the Thailand border took many months. Each day offered a challenge, and about the fourth month, we ran into heavy Khmer Rouge forces that captured us and placed us in a prison camp.

When we were first caught, the soldiers tied us to trees and left us there all day. This went on for several days before they took us into the camp. There were many buildings like chicken coops, surrounded by barbed wire and formed in a circle with armed guards standing, ready to shoot for any problem. We felt their eyes on us constantly.

There was no communication between the guards and us, unless they spoke to us. They would ask, "What do you do that is good for Ang Kai (the ruler)?"

We would have to say, "We respect him. We are loyal to him. We obey and worship him."

There were no beds, so we slept on the dirt floor. There were no sheets or pillows, and the only clothes we had were short pants, no shirt or shoes. There were 200 of us in a house, and it was crowded and smelled of sweat and filth.

The only source of water was a small pond that we also used for bathing. Seldom did we have a bath and then only for a few minutes. We were like animals sleeping.

Each group housed seven guys with a Cambodian citizen picked from the seven to manage and oversee the group. It was his job to make sure each guy worked and participated in the building of a dam.

Kha and I were in different groups, and he was picked to be the leader of his group. If, at the worksite, all seven people were not there, their leader could be shot and replaced by another guy. Kha was diligent. He and his six did what was expected to keep them and himself alive.

Everyone was expected to work, whether sick or not. Once, I was sick from starvation and could not stand, much less work. The leader tied a rope around my neck and dragged me down the road, finally throwing me to the side of the road, leaving me to die. I lay there all day until my group returned from work, helped me back to the building, and gave me a small bit of food.

Kha snuck by later and brought me food and water from his group. He could have been killed for doing that, but his love for me was stronger than his fear of being shot.

While we worked, guards with guns supervised us. Eyes were on us everywhere, all the time. Our workplace was about half a mile from where we stayed, and our job was to dig and haul dirt to the dam site.

We had a bamboo stick with baskets attached to each end, and we carried the baskets on our shoulders. It didn't matter that I was a little kid; I was expected to do what everyone else did.

A bell rang several times throughout the day, signaling the guard to check the amount of dirt we had dug up. If after the workday was done, the guard was not satisfied with the amount of work one digger had done, he would kill him and push him into a hole.

One building housed a kitchen, and there, we received one meal a day after we returned from our work. (We usually started at 5:00 a.m. and worked straight through until 6:00 p.m.) There was no break all day, just working, working.

The meals were held in shifts of about 10 groups at a time. We usually received ceramic bowls of rice and soup, and we had spoons. If the leader decided he didn't like you or felt you had not worked hard enough, he would take your food from you and give it to someone else or eat it himself. Often, I went days without having anything to eat.

One group cleaned up after the meal, and they, too, were replaced by another large group of new prisoners that had just arrived. Usually, new recruits came in every few weeks, and each of us knew that death awaited when the new ones arrived. We all knew we were replaceable.

I was one of the smaller of the boys (there were some as young as six), so I could not work as well or as hard as the others, yet the guards expected the same amount of work from me. Seldom would anyone get time off for being sick. They expected seven bodies at each work site each day, and seven bodies were what they got.

The guards abused me regularly. If I had not dug enough dirt from my hole, a guard would hit me with the butt of his metal and wood AK47 on my back. It was very painful. I suppose I was lucky he did not ram me with the attached bayonet.

Ten days after being captured, I decided I was ready to escape. There were always new prisoners coming in, and we knew the troops would kill the current inmates and fill their workloads with the new arrivals. I knew that if I stayed, I would be killed. My will to live was so strong that I began to make plans to leave. I told only Kha and asked him to come with me.

I placed myself in the corner of our housing coop, and, at night, after everyone was sleeping, I would work on digging a tunnel under the wall toward the rice field outside. It took me constant digging, using anything metal like a small hoe. I dug the dirt from the middle and packed it tightly against the sides and firmly on the floor of the tunnel.

When I didn't have a tool, I used my hands. My fingernails eventually tore off and bled. I would hide them and pick up leaves on the way to work, wet them, and make a kind of plaster to put on my fingers to hide my missing nails and protect my fingers.

After working on the tunnel each night, I would cover the space with leaves and rocks to hide it. Finally, after about three nights, I finished the tunnel, and then I notified Kha that on a certain night at a certain time, I was leaving. He agreed to come with me, so at the allotted time, he joined me. We agreed to crawl through the tunnel together. I went first, and he followed me.

The tunnel was only about 1.5 feet high and 1.5 feet wide, but we were both so skinny that, with some effort, we managed to squeeze through, staying low, so no one would see us. Sometimes, it was so tight that I had to suck in my stomach to get through part of the tunnel. Kha was also skin and bones, so he was also able to squeeze through it. Overhead, were rocks and roots, so we had to proceed slowly. However, all of my digging had made the bottom flat and smooth, so that made it easier for us to crawl.

We finally landed beside the rice field. Back when I was digging, when I got near the rice field, I veered the tunnel to the right and up the hill so that the water from the rice field would not flow back into my tunnel and flood the building. To do so would have alerted the guards of my tunnel.

Once we reached the rice field, we dropped into the water (only about three feet deep, for too much water would ruin the rice) and felt safer. One of my team members must have ratted on me because the guards became alert and began looking for us. We hid behind the bushes, and since it was night, they could not see us. We heard lots of commotion, the lights came on all over, and we heard gunshots. Someone else might have been trying to leave, too.

From the rice field, we made our way, swimming and wading, toward the Thai border where the Red Cross was waiting to help.

BUDDHISM

Prior to 1975, Buddhist monks in Cambodia numbered between 65,000 and 80,000. In 1975 when the communist Khmer Rouge took over control of Cambodia, they attempted to totally rid the country of Buddhism and very nearly succeeded.

By 1979 when Vietnam invaded Cambodia, nearly every religious intellectual or monk had been murdered or driven into exile. At the same time, nearly every Buddhist temple and library had been destroyed.

The policies of the Khmer Rouge included disrobing the monks, destroying the monasteries, and executing any uncooperative monks. This meant destroying all their Buddhist institutions. If monks did not flee and avoided execution, they lived among the Cambodians as lay people.

By the time they began to try to restore Buddhism in 1980, it is estimated that worldwide, Cambodian monks were fewer than 3,000.

Following the Vietnamese defeat of the Khmer Rouge in 1979, Buddhism in Cambodia continued to be suppressed. Then the legitimacy of the Vietnamese-backed government was challenged. Only then did Cambodia's policies toward Buddhism become more liberalized, and a group of exiled monks returned to Cambodia and began to reopen the practice of Buddhism. The government sponsored the ordination of new monks as a "public show of piety," and restrictions on ordination were lifted.

Today, Buddhism is trying to reestablish its presence in Cambodia. However, the lack of Buddhist scholars and leaders, along with the political instability there, makes this task more difficult.

The Nop family actively participated in worship, holidays, offerings, and honoring of our ancestors. When my older brother Vana became a monk, our family became closely tied to the temple and the practices of Buddhism. As a small boy, I don't remember much of the religious part, but I do remember the fun I had there, playing and spending time with Vana.

Buddhism influenced businesses with prayers and offerings for a better life and for success, and my mother actively participated in this aspect of Buddhism.

We also went to the temple three or four times a month for worship, prayer, and to make offerings. My mother was diligent in her worship.

THAILAND

The Thailand border was 306 miles "as the crow flies" from Phnom Penh. I estimate that it took us approximately five to six months to travel over 300 miles by foot to reach the border of Thailand. We ended up between Battambang and Pailin, but we went through many villages to get there.

That area is near the location of the prison camp, about 50 miles from the Thai border. We were close, but that meant nothing to those of us struggling to stay alive and avoid the soldiers.

As we drew closer to the border, we encountered fewer people traveling. The officers were killing people right up to the border. They would hide in holes and have their guns ready, mowing people down like rats. There were even times when the troops actually crossed the border and shot Cambodians on the Thailand side. On occasion, the Thai troops would shoot back at them.

Finally, we came closer to the border. There were fewer people since many had been killed or few were there to cross the border. At one village, we saw people with motorbikes, some with wagons attached to the bike in the back.

They offered a ride to the border in exchange for gold. They did not want money but would barter for gold or silver. We had nothing. We begged them to take us, but they were determined to help only those who had gold or silver.

The bargain was for an ounce of gold, for which they would drive us to the border. One woman took pity on me and offered to pay a driver to take me for half an ounce of gold which was all she had. However, he would take only me. Kha couldn't come. I said I wouldn't go without Kha. He insisted that I go, that he would catch up with me by walking.

I finally agreed to go, and we took off, me in the back wagon with the driver on his bike. As we pulled away, Kha jumped into the wagon and hid. We went about 15 miles when another biker told my driver that Kha had jumped onboard. My driver pulled over and kicked Kha off.

It was 22 miles to the border of Thailand. Kha and I agreed to meet once we arrived there. He would walk the rest of the way while I continued on the bike for another 15 miles. The driver eventually stopped and made me get off, saying he would not go any further.

I kept walking toward Thailand alone, and when it was evening, I came upon a train station. It was quite dark. The doors of the station were open, and I was exhausted. I went into the dark room and saw many people in the seats around the room. I found a seat and collapsed into a deep sleep.

I woke up when the sun rose, looked around, and felt terrified to see that everyone in the room was dead. Flies were buzzing everywhere. Apparently, the soldiers had gotten there the day before and killed everyone and had moved on. I was in shock, and the terror of the situation rushed at me.

It seemed that everywhere I went, similar activities had taken place, sparing me. I don't know why I never stopped a bullet, never stepped on a mine, and often heard bullets whizzed past my head. I just kept running.

Bodies were in all conditions, with heads blown off, intestines falling out, limbs hanging loose, everyone dead. I took two pieces of meat from one of the bodies, carried it with me, and when I could, I stopped, built a fire, cooked and ate the two pieces. I was starving, and, at that point, my thought was that I would survive.

After I ate, I felt more strength and moved forward to the border.

THE BORDER

When I reached Thailand, the grass was green, the palm trees were abundant, and there was a quiet that was new to me and my journey. Once I crossed into Thailand, I felt the fear leave me a little.

I was still uncertain what to do or where to go since Kha had not joined me yet. I followed other people, and we entered into the International Border, a large area heading into the actual border to Thailand. It served as a holding camp, and I stayed there for several months.

Other countries had donated items through their disaster relief programs, and many Cambodian people could set up tents or little markets where they sold food, mainly rice, sandwich-type meals, and chicken. They required Baht (Thai money) for the food they sold. I had no money, so I would go around and pick up rice or food off the ground, dropped as people stood around and ate.

Without Kha there, I was lonely and slept on the ground near other people. After about 10 days, Kha showed up. He was so thin and haggard! I hardly recognized him.

"Is that you, Kha?' I asked with some concern.

He admitted that it was him, and we were happy to be back together. I showed him around and helped him get some food.

The Red Cross gave everyone packets of rice, dry fish, sardines, and water. I had to make sure to be there at a certain time when the Red Cross rolled in and gave us these packets. If I was late, I missed the handout for the day. When I first arrived, the Red Cross gave me some medicine, but one time only. I don't know what it was, but I took it gladly.

While I was searching for food and finding my way around this enclosure, a Cambodian woman, Sovan Teng, approached me and asked if I needed help. She was with her daughter, Ash, who was about my age. I gladly said yes, and she took Kha and me under her wing. She lived in a small house within the enclosure and invited Kha and me to stay with her. I was no longer starving, but I was always hungry.

Our life got better around 1979. Sovan Teng then was relocated to the refugee camp called Khao I Dang, located on hundreds of acres of land. There were barbed wire fences around the camp with Thai guards with rifles. Their purpose was to keep Cambodians in the camp and not allow them to leave and mingle into their country.

Sovan Teng took us with her, and shortly after that, she received a sponsor and prepared to leave for the United States. She applied for herself and two children and asked me to go with them. However, Kha could not go, so I decided to stay with him. I found out later she made it to the United States, and we were in touch for a while once I arrived here.

During my stay in the camp, one of the Thai officers befriended me. He looked out for me like a big brother and gave me freedom to go out of the camp and shop for things for myself.

At one point, he left to visit his family for a week and put me in charge of his post, gun and all. I agreed to let some of the Cambodians leave to gather firewood or get food and go fishing. He trusted me that much, and I worked hard to keep his trust.

He lived in Bangkok, was a captain in the army, and he was big in the service. He even took me to visit his family there once. They liked me and wanted me to stay in Thailand with them. Kha was invited, too, but he was more cautious, and he decided to remain in the camp.

However, the Thai people did not like or trust Cambodians due to the past history of wars, so I felt it would be better for me not to stay. (Darker-skinned Cambodian people stand out there. The Thai have lighter skin and are taller, due to merging with other cultures in the past).

When the captain returned from Bangkok, he would sometimes bring us items of clothes or shoes. When Sovan left to go to the United

States, this officer took us to the group home, an orphanage, and told the people in charge, "Take good care of these boys." He also advised us to go to America as our choice for relocation. We took his advice. Our second choice was Canada.

The captain later left since a new group of officers came every month to watch over the camp. I do not know his name, but I would have liked to let him know we made it OK.

There were hundreds of kids in the orphanage. Workers with UNICEF helped us fill out papers and gave us a choice of a number of places to go. After a lot of discussion, Kha and I decided to go to the United States.

There were two sides to the process. Side one included completing paperwork, getting our pictures taken, and receiving a document allowing us to enter the United States. They advised us to lower our real age by about three years to qualify for the minors' program. My birthday is March 2, 1971. Kha's is April 22, 1968. At that time, I was around 10 and Kha was about 14. They put me down as 7 and Kha,11.

Every day, the orphanage put up a list of the names of kids and where they had been assigned sponsors. We looked every day, and one day, our names were on the board. We were going to Roanoke, Virginia!

Side two included getting a haircut, obtaining shoes, being fitted for clothes (a coat, a sweater, suit pants – I still have those pants – jeans, shirts, and a toothbrush and comb.) Then they gave us the official paper with stamps on it that would allow us to get into the United States. They told us to keep this paper with us at all times.

LEAVING THAILAND

Finally, the time came for us to leave the refugee camp. The staff at UNICEF drove us to Bangkok, and we boarded our first plane. We were scared but also excited. We had no idea what was ahead. I felt very shy and afraid, but it was a different kind of fear. No one was trying to kill us now, but we didn't know what to expect. I think I was more nervous than afraid.

They served us food: a sandwich in a plastic container. We had no idea what it was or how to open the box. We were used to rice and soup! And then there was the bathroom on the plane, a very strange place. We were getting a quick view of differences in the two cultures, and we had a long way to go!

We slept most of the time on the trip. For the first time in a long time, we could relax and sleep. After about six hours, we landed in Japan and stayed for a short time. However, there the food was familiar. We got rice and our kind of food! It was a welcome change.

Next we boarded a 747 Pan Am (I remember clearly the name of that plane)! We were quickly seated in this big plane. We were also surprised that the ride was so smooth that we couldn't feel it move! We were more relaxed and not so scared.

The flight to California would take 12 hours, and we again fell into a deep sleep, only waking up when the stewards tapped us on the shoulder to serve us food. (This American food would take some getting used to, but we were happy to have any food.)

ARRIVING IN VIRGINIA

We landed in California at night, and UNICEF staff with interpreters greeted us. We were put in a room in the hotel and spent the next week there. I think there were about 400 people, many Cambodians, other minors, too. It was there that we prepared to go to our family in Roanoke. I don't remember a lot about that time, except we played basketball and learned who our American family would be.

When we got ready to leave, UNICEF staff called out, "Two minors for Roanoke, Virginia" and we boarded the plane. We had no idea where this place was or what it was like. We knew it had mountains and snow.

I don't remember much about the flight from California to Virginia or whether we landed somewhere in between. It seems we flew directly to Virginia from California, but I don't think that is true. I don't remember if there were other minors on the plane with us, going other places.

We were some of the earliest Cambodians to arrive with the Refugee Unaccompanied Minors Program. We had been told about a couple with one girl that lived in the country, and they would be happy to have us come live with them and be our foster parents.

We arrived in Virginia late one evening, landing in the Roanoke airport, where we met our foster father, Cody, Chamron (our Cambodian interpreter and counselor), and Robin, our social worker. Since we arrived at night, we could not see what Roanoke or Virginia looked like. I was again scared, not knowing if the foster family would be nice. For the first six months, I was shy and nervous. I couldn't speak English, so mainly I was quiet and kept to myself.

A day or so after we arrived, Cody called us to the window, and we saw snow for the first time! We ran right out but had to go back in to get our boots and coats. It was wonderful! We could have played all day, but because it was so cold, we went in after four hours.

I didn't like all the spaghetti, noodles, and mashed potatoes. Sometimes, I would eat it, and other times, I didn't. Later, we had rice and fried or baked chicken, and I liked that.

Since Kha was older, he had more issues adjusting. (As an adult, he told people he had a lot of PTSD, so he moved to a group home.) About 18 months later, to be closer to Kha, I moved into Roanoke.

And so began our move into this country, learning the language, going to school, meeting other Cambodian kids, as well as those coming from Laos and Vietnam. In the RUMP program, we participated in native dances, native music, learning about each other's culture, having get-togethers with everyone, and serving food native to our individual cultures. The RUMP program put together a cookbook. We took a bus trip to visit a Buddhist temple. Our foster parents gave us many opportunities to learn about various things.

About 18 months after Kha left, I joined Joyce's family, and they became my American family. A new family, a new country, a new language, a new life. That is when I moved from hell to heaven.

Now I have told my story.

Vany Nop a few months after arriving in Roanoke, VA

Joyce with Kha on arrival in Roanoke, VA, in December 1982

*Group outing to Buddhist temple in Richmond, VA
(Cambodian, Vietnamese, Lao) with staff*

Cambodian dance

Buddhist part of ANGKOR WAT ancient temple –
Vany returned to Cambodia in 2013

Vany on horseback in front of the ancient ANGKOR WAT TEMPLE in Cambodia

Made in the USA
Middletown, DE
24 August 2024

59271564R00033